KEEPING SCORE

BOOKS BY ROBERT HAMBLIN

Poetry

Perpendicular Rain   (1986)

From the Ground Up: Poems of One Southerner's Passage to Adulthood   (1992)

Mind the Gap: Poems by an American in London   (2004)

Keeping Score: Sports Poems for Every Season   (2007)

Autobiography

Bless You, My Father   (2006)

Biography

Win or Win: A Season with Ron Shumate   (1993)

Faulkner Studies

Selections from the William Faulkner Collection of Louis Daniel
    Brodsky: A Descriptive Catalog *(with Louis Daniel Brodsky)*   (1978)

Faulkner: A Comprehensive Guide to the Brodsky Collection
    (five volumes, with Louis Daniel Brodsky)   (1982–88)

Country Lawyer and Other Stories for the Screen *(with Louis Daniel Brodsky)*   (1987)

Stallion Road: A Screenplay by William Faulkner *(with Louis Daniel Brodsky)*   (1989)

A William Faulkner Encyclopedia *(with Charles A. Peek)*   (1999)

Teaching Faulkner: Approaches and Methods *(with Stephen Hahn)*   (2000)

Faulkner in the Twenty-First Century *(with Ann J. Abadie)*   (2003)

A Companion to Faulkner Studies *(with Charles A. Peek)*   (2004)

KEEPING SCORE

SPORTS POEMS
FOR EVERY SEASON

ROBERT HAMBLIN

TIME BEING BOOKS
POETRY IN SIGHT AND SOUND

An imprint of Time Being Press
St. Louis, Missouri

Copyright © 2007 by Robert Hamblin

All rights reserved under International and Pan-American Copyright Conventions. No part of this book shall be reproduced in any form (except by reviewers for the public press) without written permission from the publisher:

Time Being Books®
10411 Clayton Road
St. Louis, Missouri 63131

Time Being Books® is an imprint of Time Being Press®, St. Louis, Missouri.

Time Being Press® is a 501(c)(3) not-for-profit corporation.

Time Being Books® volumes are printed on acid-free paper.

ISBN 978-1-56809-114-3 (paperback)

Library of Congress Cataloging-in-Publication Data:

Hamblin, Robert.
    Keeping score : sports poems for every season / by Robert Hamblin — 1st ed.
        p. cm.
      ISBN-13: 978-1-56809-114-3 (pbk. : alk. paper)
        1. Sports — Poetry. 2. Seasons — Poetry. I. Title.
    PS3608.A54944 K44 2007
    811'.6 — 22
                                                    2007011433

Cover design by Jeff Hirsch
Cover photos copyrighted by and reprinted with permission of Lew Portnoy and Michael Burton
Book design and typesetting by Trilogy Mattson

Manufactured in the United States of America

First Edition, first printing (2007)

ACKNOWLEDGMENTS

Several of the poems included in this volume — some in slightly different versions — previously appeared in other publications: "Half-Court Advantage," in *Arete: The Journal of Sport Literature*; "Big Apple," "Basketball Suite," "Pick and Roll," and "The Way to Watch a Football Game," in *Aethlon: The Journal of Sport Literature*; "For Dal, on the Fourth of July," in *Spitball*; "Groundskeepers: Opening Day" and "Mr. October," in *Elysian Fields Quarterly*; "Autumn at Woodland Hills Country Club," "On the Death of the Evansville University Basketball Team in a Plane Crash, December 13, 1977," "To an Athlete Dying Old," and "Running: Cape Girardeau, November 1993," in *The Cape Rock*; and "Requital," in *From the Ground Up* (Time Being Books, 1992). I wish to express my sincere appreciation to each of these publishers for permission to reprint those poems here.

I also wish to acknowledge the encouragement and assistance I have received from my friends and colleagues in the Sport Literature Association and with *Aethlon: The Journal of Sport Literature*, the academic organization and journal that, for a quarter century now, have promoted the creation and study of the literature of sport. I have especially benefited from my personal and professional friendship with Jack Higgs, Lyle Olsen, Fred Boe, Don Johnson, David Vanderwerken, Eric Solomon, Richard Crepeau, Ed Sims, Judy Hakola, H. R. Stoneback, Tim Morris, and Joyce Duncan, all of whom are among the pioneering figures in the field of sport literature.

My debt to the poets published in the pages of *Aethlon* during the two decades in which I served as its poetry editor is incalculable. Their work has been an ongoing source of pleasure, insight, and craftsmanship.

I also want to thank Jerry Call, the managing editor of Time Being Books, for his careful and insightful reading of the manuscript of this volume and for his many fine suggestions for improvements.

Finally, as always, I express my deepest love and gratitude to my wife, Kaye, for her continuing inspiration and support.

To L. D. Brodsky,
poet, scholar, athlete,
and best friend

CONTENTS

Prologue

Now a Fastball, Now a Curve

The Way to Watch a Football Game

The Pole Vaulter and Other Heroes

Half-Court Advantage

KEEPING SCORE

(*) This symbol is used to indicate that a stanza has been divided because of pagination.

PROLOGUE

The Dumb Jock Replies

You say we're dumb.
But we know some things
you'll never know.

Like how the solid feel
of bat on ball
electrifies the hands, arms,
shoulders, hips, legs, feet,
engineering chemistries
into stand-up triples.

Or the pure poetry
of a pulling guard
planting a shoulder
into a linebacker's belly,
freeing the runner
for the end zone.

Or the computed perfection
of a crossover dribble,
setting loose the body's move
past a defender
and ending in the musical arc
of a jump shot finding the net.

Or the geometric ecstasy
of sprinting down the field
to deflect a corner kick
with a head shot
that explodes past the goalie's
diving arms.

If you're so smart
why don't you know these things?
Don't those books you read
teach you that all knowledge
is grounded in the body,
begins there and must end there?

You make too much of mind.
Look at the world since Freud
diddled with thought:
conflicted, confused, paranoid,
sick, suicidal.

Jocks know not to think
in the middle of the backswing
or when the rocketing pitch
or serve comes at you.

It's the body
that demands survival —
how to find your way
back to the huddle
after having your bell rung,
how to summon aching knees
and burning lungs
to finish the race.

You won't find jocks
hanging over the rails of bridges,
being begged not to jump.

And what's more,
which you library types
will never understand,
we get the dates.

NOW A FASTBALL,
NOW A CURVE

Clear Channel Stations

Nighttime brought the larger world:
KDKA Pittsburgh, WGN Chicago,
KMOX St. Louis, WCKY Cincinnati,
WJR Detroit.

Ballroom orchestras that played
past midnight, New Year's Eve specials
on Buick Roadmasters if only you lived
close enough to drive there.

But best of all, baseball,
the hand on the lighted dial
moving east to west,
following the time zone which ended,
in those pre-expansion days, in St. Louis,
beyond which stretched nothing but desert.
The voices of Bob Prince, Jack Brickhouse,
Harry Caray, and Ernie Harwell
splitting the distant dark
like a Robin Roberts fastball
or a Ralph Kiner home run.

The local station was a rainout:
the price of cotton, a gospel quartet,
the daily swap shop, rolling out
the tarp at five o'clock.

Summer of '51

That was the year
he discovered baseball,
not the imitation kind
he would later play in dimly lit parks
with dirt infields all across
north Mississippi, but real baseball
that fired his imagination
and dreams, brought down
to him in magical voices
over airways from heaven:
Al Helfer, Harry Caray, Red Barber,
Mel Allen, Lindsey Nelson.

It was his grandfather
who introduced him to the game.
He came to live with them
after his wife died, taking up residence
in the "south room"
of the large, rambling house
and bringing with him an ancient, wrinkled face,
a humped back, a feeble gait
supported by a walking stick,
an old man's absolute right
to listen to every baseball game
he could find on the radio dial,
and an unconditional love
for a twelve-year-old boy who,
born late to aging, hardworking parents,
ached for companionship.

His grandfather was a Cardinals fan,
but the boy fell in love with the Dodgers.
He would never forget the day:
the season barely begun, an afternoon broadcast
on *Mutual's Game of the Day*,
the Cubs leading the Dodgers by seven runs
until a barrage of home runs
turned defeat into sudden, glorious victory.
It was love at first hearing,
*

and for the rest of that year,
he schooled himself in the fabulous lore
of Ebbets Field and Flatbush,
recited the litany of his heroes —
Snider, Hodges, Campanella, Reese,
Robinson, Furillo, Cox, Roe,
Erskine, Newcombe.

His grandfather died
in the middle of the season, on June 28.
That night his body was laid out for viewing
in the south room while family,
neighbors, and friends attended the wake.
The boy moved solemnly among the crowd,
the women gathered in the kitchen,
serving food, or sitting quietly
in the living room,
the men seated on the porch
or standing in the yard,
some wearing coats and ties,
others in bib overalls.
Strangely, there was no talk of baseball at all.
The next afternoon the boy
held tightly to his mother's hand
as he watched
his grandfather being laid to rest
in the family plot in the rural cemetery
with the biblical name, Jericho,
where the walls came tumbling down.

That same year, on October 3,
he persuaded his mother to allow him
to skip school to listen to the final playoff game
between the Dodgers and the Giants.
Transported on the voice of Russ Hodges
to a bleacher seat in the Polo Grounds,
he delighted as the Dodgers
took a three-run lead into the ninth,
agonized as Big Newk faltered,
*

prayed for Branca as he walked
from the bullpen to the mound,
despaired when Thomson hit the homer
and the radio screamed:
"The Giants win the pennant!
The Giants win the pennant!
The Giants win the pennant!"
Then, for the second time that summer,
the boy cried.

Forever after
he was hooked on baseball,
and the Dodgers,
playing the game every chance he got,
following his heroes on the radio
(and soon on TV), reading box scores
in the Tupelo and Memphis papers,
even subscribing to *The Sporting News.*
And all the while he thought
it was baseball he loved.
Only years later would he realize
it was the voices on the radio,
disembodied words
from angelic messengers
delivering to his very door
evocative images of a mythic desire
stretching far beyond his childhood home,
and those precious, doomed evenings
spent in the company of a gentle old man
on a rotting front porch, the sounds
of radio baseball floating
through an open window,
a soft, seamless moon climbing
the eastern sky like a Gil Hodges homer
rising through the Brooklyn night,
and thousands of sparkling fireflies,
wistful pulsings of a youthful heart,
dividing the long darkness
with their bright, spontaneous,
silent cheering.

Stickball, Country Style

After the radio voices
and the studio-manufactured
crowd noises had faded,
he would go outside
with his makeshift bat —
the handle of one of his mother's
discarded brooms or mops —
and hit fungoes with small rocks
picked, like unopened bolls of cotton,
from the gravel road
that ran beside his house.

Often, he would play
imaginary games, pitting
his favorite team, the Dodgers,
against Ewell "The Whip" Blackwell
or Robin Roberts.
Grounders or pop flies
that failed to clear the road
were outs, flies landing between
the ditch and the chain-link fence
surrounding the Presbyterian cemetery
across the road were singles,
over the near fence a double,
past the angel high atop the Agnew
family monument a triple.
Over the back fence, clearing
the cemetery entirely,
was a home run.

He always played fair:
for Reese and Cox, singles hitters,
he selected rocks that stayed
close to home, large ones
that stung the hands and barely left
the ground, or thin, waferlike ones
that zinged through the air,
then hooked or sliced to earth
like a shot quail.
*

The smooth, round stones
that could fly straight and far
like pigeons he reserved
for the power hitters —
Snider, Hodges, Campanella.
He cheated only in this respect:
all the perfectly shaped agates
went to Hodges, his idol.

During the '52 Series, while
a Brooklyn priest held a special mass
to pray for Gil to break his slump,
the boy, offering prayers of another sort,
powered rock after rock over the dead
in a north Mississippi cemetery.

Years later, a man, though still
a boy where baseball was concerned,
he stopped at a corner newsstand
in St. Louis and read the headline
that Gil Hodges had died.
Stunned, he caught
in his mind's eye a fleeting glimpse,
tangible and real as a child's bad dream,
of a hard, round stone falling to earth,
among tombstones engraved with names
he thought he had forgotten forever:
Leslie, Huckaby, Hickey, Bryson, Hill.

A Hero for All Seasons

I remember Eddie Yost:

Who raised the base on balls
to the level of art.

Who took batting practice
to practice not to hit.

Who once fouled off nineteen
third strikes to earn a walk.

Who persuaded kids too small
for football and too short
for basketball
that littl'uns could also be big'uns.

Coach

After the women
had had their way with us
(which took years)
they led us down the hall,
to Coach Wilemon,
and left us there.

His office
was the wire cage
just off the gym floor,
which also served
as the equipment room.

"The first person who comes in here,"
he warned, "will go back out
without a pecker."

Even the principal stayed away.

The gym was always
dark and musty,
smelling of mildewing sweats
and old tennis shoes.
Coach Wilemon's voice
was as huge and offensive
as his obscene belly.

Johnny Williams peed
in his pants the first day.

"Everybody on this line!"
Coach screamed.
"America is producing
a whole generation
of weaklings.
But we're gonna change that,
right here and now.
When you hear this whistle,
goddammit, RUN!"

We all ran.
Some of us never stopped.

Now a Fastball, Now a Curve

Truth sometimes
is undeniable and direct,
a high, hard fastball
under your chin,
landing you on your back
in the dirt
at the catcher's feet,
or a sweeping curve
spinning off
the outside corner,
clearly out of reach.

But often,
and always
in clutch situations
that matter most,
it's a splitter,
rocketing toward you
like an unmistakable
two-seamer
heading straight
into your power alley,
then dropping,
unexpectedly
and unavoidably,
into the inescapable
surprise and mystery
of the unknown.

Walking back
to the dugout,
looking for the hole
in your bat
that left questions
stranded on every base,
you know that belief
has been fooled again
into disbelief.

For Dal, on the Fourth of July

We envied your fluid,
compact swing that sent
singles and doubles exploding
to all fields like bottle rockets,

And your accurate, pellet-gun aim
that toppled runners off bases
like toy pigeons
from carnival shelves.

Even then, as boys, we all
knew you were the only one
good enough to play college ball
and have a chance at the pros.

But mostly we envied you
your father. In summer league
he manned first while you caught
or played right. Middle-aged
father and teenage son, together
on the same team and the same field,
the true American myth
of what baseball is all about.

Once, I remember,
in the dugout between innings,
he took me aside
and, wrapping his arms around me
from behind, and laying his hands
on mine, showed me how
to step into the pitch
and guide my bat in a level arc
through the hitting zone.

It always seemed to the rest of us
that, with a father like that,
we could hit line drives forever.

Swoboda

This is the first time. Nothing can ever be as
sweet again.
— Ron Swoboda, after the 1969 World Series

Say "Swoboda,"
and every baseball fan
will instantly see
that perennial October replay
of an outfielder lunging,
diving, body parallel
to earth and air, arm and glove
outstretched, clutching
the low, sinking line drive
and miraculously holding the ball
as his chest, face, body
strike the ground.
The greatest catch
in World Series history.

And those older than Astroturf
and instant replay
will recall the details:
the fourth game of the '69 Series,
the Miracle Mets up two games to one,
the Orioles threatening with two on
in the top of the ninth,
Brooks Robinson at bat,
and Swoboda, in right, cheating in
for a play at the plate,
not knowing that those few inches
had moved him beyond time,
into immortality.

And real aficionados may reflect
on the wonderfully comic irony
in the event:
how, in the city of Dimaggio,
Mantle, and Mays,
those matchless wonders,
*

one of the hapless Mets,
a player brought up too soon
by an ancient and desperate Stengel,
and then, platooned by Hodges,
never allowed to develop
the confidence required for stardom,
would be the one chosen
to be the darling of destiny.

But I go them all one better.
It is a late spring day in 1961
in Sparrows Point, Maryland,
almost dusk, and an overgrown,
muscular 17-year-old schoolboy
is standing in for batting practice
against a rookie assistant coach
(by profession an English teacher)
only two years removed from his final,
indisputable failure at a tryout camp.
All the other players have long since
departed for dinner and dates.
Neighborhood children, happy
for their chance to play, chase down
the batted balls and return them
to the mound.

In the near darkness
you can hear the crack of the bat
and just make out the flight
of the ball to deepest center.
The pitcher winds again.
The hitter waits, silhouetted
in rough-sculptured relief,
bat arched in readiness,
aiming toward the sky.

American Pastime

All day long
I've eagerly anticipated
seeing the great Koufax
pitch against the Cardinals,
and now, after rushing home from work
and driving two and a half hours,
I'm planted in a box seat
along the first base line,
scorecard in hand,
awaiting the first pitch.

Two guys sitting beside me
are also excitedly awaiting
the start of the game,
but, as I soon discover,
for an altogether different reason.

Bet you a dollar
the first pitch is a strike,
one says as Maury Wills stands in
to lead off against Al Jackson.
You're on, the other says,
and thus begins
their game within the game.

And for nine innings,
as Koufax winds that magic arm
and hurls mitt-popping fastballs
and his best curve balls of the season
past befuddled Cardinal hitters,
wagers are tossed back and forth
like fielders playing catch.

Two dollars says McCarver will strike out.
Bet you Roseboro will hit a fly ball.
Give me 3-1 odds that Wills will steal
on this at bat?
Bet you fifty cents that Cepeda
will get a base hit.
*

And even this,
as Dal Maxvill lobs the ball
toward the mound
after catching a popup for the third out:
I'll bet you fifty cents
that it'll stop on dirt.

I try to concentrate on the game,
fix my gaze on the marvelous
and heroic Koufax
as he overpowers batter after batter,
sending them, head down
and bat still in hand,
back to the dugout,
his artistry made even more brilliant
and awesome by the knowledge
that after the game he will sit for an hour
with his arthritic elbow encased in rubber
and buried in a bucket of ice.

The Dodgers win, 2-1.
Only a Curt Flood homer
enables the Cardinals to avoid
the shutout.
It's Koufax's 26th win of the year.
He fans 13, becoming the first pitcher
in baseball history
to strike out 300 batters
in three different seasons.
He K's the side
in the fourth and sixth innings
and over one stretch throws
17 consecutive strikes.

All lost on the men sitting beside me:
craft perfected through long struggle,
beauty made more beautiful by pain,
grace born of trial and sweat.

There are two outs in the ninth
as Mike Shannon strides to the plate.
You owe me $3.50.
I'll bet you double or nothing
that the last out is a ground ball.

Groundskeepers: Opening Day

Tell me why,
if you can,
my favorite time
at the ballpark
is on opening day,
when the groundskeepers
take center stage
at home plate
to line the batter's box:

The crowd
leaning into the season
like a cleanup hitter
sitting on a 3-1 fastball,
the players
poised on the dugout steps
awaiting the umpire's call,
like God's
in that other garden,
to the dazzling possibilities
to be played out
within foul lines
stretching to infinity.

Robert Freeman

Busch Stadium, 1970,
a Sunday afternoon game,
Cards versus the Pirates.

In the bottom of the seventh
Torre drives a high fly
to deep right. Clemente
back pedals gracefully,
casually pulls the ball
out of the air,
then unleashes a laser throw
to third to hold Javier
on second. Amazed,
I follow the ball
splitting the air all the way
to Hebner on the fly.
The crowd, in concert,
exhales a loud "Oooh!"
in admiration.

It's my first time to see
the incomparable Clemente,
but immediately I'm aware
that I've seen that throw before.
But where? For the rest
of the game, and on the drive home,
I search my memory for the moment.

And then I remember.

Early 1950s.
A dusty Mississippi summer.
A cow-pasture baseball game
between two Negro teams.
A white boy too young to play,
even had the teams been white,
is among the spectators.
One of the players, the best,
and the only one in full uniform,
wears number 42 on his back.
*

"Robert Freeman," the boy's father
tells him. Then somewhere
in the course of the game
Freeman cuts loose a throw
from deep center that clears
the catcher's head by a good ten feet,
sails over the makeshift backstop,
and disappears into the woods
ringing the field.
The boy had never seen
a baseball thrown so far,
and he would not see
a matching throw until that day
when he'd watch Clemente
let one fly in St. Louis.

Sometimes I wonder
what happened to Robert Freeman.
I know he never made it
to the big leagues;
no Mississippi black did in those days,
unlike Don Blassingame,
the white kid from Corinth,
who played second base
for the Cardinals.
Did Freeman go Up North,
to Chicago maybe,
like so many blacks of his generation,
searching for a life to match his name?
I wonder if he ever saw Clemente play.
Did he ever sit, as I have done,
in the bleachers of a major league park
and watch dozens of outfielders,
though few with the arm
of a Robert Freeman?
Or was he swallowed up —
talent, potential, ambition,
all — by the Jim Crow South,
his only autograph an errant throw
still sailing in a white man's memory
in the lost Mississippi sunlight?

Hammerin' Hank: #715

"I never saw them,"
you said later of the two college kids,
both white, who climbed down
from the bleachers and trotted alongside
as you rounded third and headed
for baseball immortality.

And no wonder.
You weren't about to let two honkies
intrude upon this moment.
Not after the miles and years
you traveled to run these 90 feet.

So what if you were now
the toast of Atlanta,
the most Southern of all cities,
and to whites as well as blacks.
So what if no hotel clerk,
minor or major league,
could anymore dare to refuse you
service with your white teammates,
send you across town to sleep and eat
in the colored section of town.
So what if even those fans
who once wore hoods
and voted for Lester Maddox
would now be more than happy
to invite you home for dinner,
let you sign an autograph or two for the kids.

Could that atone for the long,
lonely youth in segregated Mobile,
the long bus rides in the Negro League,
the boos and obscenities in the Sally League,
the cold, condescending stares in Milwaukee,
and now, finally, as you approached the summit
no one was expected to climb,
the death threats contained in letters
that claimed "no nigger will ever break
the Babe's record"?

They were all determined to make you
stay in your place,
admit you were different.

Well, you were different,
you certainly showed them that,
though not in the way they anticipated,
or preferred. Sullen and speechless,
you answered them all with your bat.
It helped that the ball was white.

Turning Forty

In a game of one-cat
Stephen
lofts a pop fly
over my head.

I turn and run,
clumsily, painfully,
straining forgetful limbs
in a comic dance,
leaping,
stretching the gloved hand
beyond my body,
feeling the awkward
surprise of ball
settle into the pocket
of the mitt.

I hit the ground,
a spry seventeen-year-old
shortstop,
spin and rocket
a perfect throw
to Richard,
doubling the runner off first.

Trotting, ageless,
to the bench,
I warm to the applause
of appreciative fans
and Coach's happy
slap on the back.

Thanks, son,
I needed that.

Mr. October

Brock, Carew, Boggs,
Yount, Gwynn, Sandberg:
those impressive career numbers,
compiled, admirably,
through longevity
may win over our heads,
but never our souls.

We'll give you a pedestal
in the Hall, but not
in our hearts.

No, in real life,
where most of our hits
are dribblers between short and third,
we'd trade any two players
with perfect Roto League stats
for one Reggie Jackson:

Mr. October,
who arrived every season
just in the nick of time
to pull us back from the fall
of the year, when our lives
seemed about to descend forevermore
into acceptance and defeat,

And, with one gigantic swing,
one orgastic explosion of the spirit,
blasted the lights out
in the deepest part of the darkest night,
loosing our dreams from narrow infields
of desire into the seamless, celestial
orbit of the home run.

Year after yearning year
we rode that towering swing
all the way to April.

Slo-Pitch Pitcher

Ages ago,
so the record book says,
it was strength vs. strength,
challenging all sluggers,
confidently mixing fastballs,
curves, and sliders,
and aiming a high hard one
under the chin of any
who dared to dig in
and crowd the plate.
Our own game to win or lose,
as that great sportswriter, Shakespeare,
might have said.

But today,
on the far side of innocence,
suited up for this last stop
before retirement,
more often victim than hero,
one's options are limited:
a reverse or forward spin,
varying the arc,
teasing .800 hitters
into lunging after
low outside floaters
or overreaching for the fence.

Sooner or later
all strike zones narrow
to a wing and a prayer,
and making damned sure
you have a wide-ranging shortstop
and a left fielder
with a rocket for an arm.

At the Ballpark

Busch Stadium, St. Louis, August 28, 2001

Where it all begins
with the CEO of Sturdy Paper Bags, Inc.
throwing out the first pitch
while all his friends and associates
huddle around Fredbird
and the rookie reliever just up from Memphis
for photographs for their office walls,
and the combined children's choirs
from a dozen elementary schools
fill the outfield to sing
the National Anthem,

And where, once the game is underway,
fans check the huge message board
to see if Baptist groups in attendance
outnumber the Catholics
and who has 50th wedding anniversaries
and 80th birthdays
and if this is the night
that George will propose to Meredith,
or look for themselves
on the big screen among replay
after replay of the greatest catches
or the funniest bloopers of the season,
or live shots of other fans
singing karaoke or guessing the number of people
in the stands or playing
baseball trivia or lunging
after rolled-up tee shirts
catapulted into the stands
by lovely, long-legged girls
wearing shorts and halters,

And where beyond the outfield fences
children swing on junglegyms
while their parents
gather in the company boxes
*

and order more beer and pretzels
and read the day's performance of the Dow
posted (courtesy of Edward Jones)
on the scoreboard high above center field,
waiting for another fireworks display
following a home run
or the airplane looping overhead
for Big Ed's Used Cars,

Yet still where at least a few of us
revel in a base runner
alertly moving from first to third,
or the shortstop edging closer
to second base,
or the relief pitcher
leaning in for his sign,
or the on-deck batter signaling
the runner to slide.

"You Gotta Believe!"

The voice on the line,
quiet and somber,
is Swoboda's,
informing me that Tug McGraw,
his teammate with the Mets,
is lying in a hospital
in Clearwater, Florida,
cancerous tumors,
perhaps inoperable,
invading his brain.
This time it'll take
a real miracle.

I imagine phone calls like this
from all the old Mets and Phillies
and their thousands of fans
going out, like prayers,
from earth to satellite and back,
posters lifted high above heads
in every stadium and park and home,
begging for relief.

Oh God, manager
of all pitchers, hitters, and fielders,
owner of the great game itself,
visit Your servant Tug
on the mound of his distress,
put your hand upon his shoulder
and speak to him encouragement
and strength to face down
and defeat this disease
as he once did opposing batters,
save him now as he once
saved others.

As all the old players,
still tough in the clutch,
rally in spirit to the aid
of their teammate and friend,
*

I replay the memory of a young pitcher
blowing a third strike
past the hitter
with the bases loaded,
then striding confidently
to the dugout, with every step
slapping his glove against his side.

Box Score

They've ruined box scores,
like so much of the game.
Too many details,
summaries,
every inning made as literal
as an instant replay.

Used to be boxes
were pure poetry:
no clutter, just the essence,
lines and rows of numbers
and names
as balanced and musical
as a sonnet,
the last out
or the winning hit,
no less than the memory
of the smell
of a hotdog
or the cheers of the crowd,
a construct of the imagination.

It never was the game we loved,
but the poetry of the game.

At the Baseball Hall of Fame

A boy, I never thought I'd visit here,
Cooperstown being about as close
to Mississippi as the moon.

But here I am, fifty years later,
reading the plaques
of my boyhood heroes —
Reese, Robinson, Campanella, Snider —
wandering from room to room,
looking at bats, balls, gloves, caps
used by Cobb and Speaker and Dimaggio
and Koufax and Gwynn,
watching replays of Willie's great catch
and Maz's winning homer
and Ozzie's backflip,
viewing the display of the home run race
between McGwire and Sosa.

Kaye and I have come here
on our way to Niagara Falls,
another place I've never visited before,
and she has graciously granted me
this day to spend with my other love,
my first, and the one she's shared me with
through all the years.

But I quickly discover
the old magic is gone,
a long affair of the heart turned stale.
Perhaps I waited too long,
but I knew it would be like this
as soon as I saw Joe Pepitone
camped out near the front entrance
signing autographs for ten bucks a throw
and Pete Rose hawking memorabilia
in one of the shops just down the street.
Moneychangers and crooks in the temple
and no angry messiah anywhere to be seen.

So I walk hurriedly through the exhibits,
thinking I'm ready to move on —
until I discover the section devoted
to the play-by-play broadcasters of my youth,
and once again those legendary voices
reclaim for me poignant memories of people,
places, and events from my boyhood,
and of the game I will always love.

THE WAY TO WATCH A FOOTBALL GAME

Big Apple

From our vantage point as seventh-graders,
looking up and dreaming, you had it all:
the prettiest girl in the entire school,
hero status as the starting tailback,
a swaggering, confident manner that made
everyone, even the adults who should
have known better, believe in your invincibility.
And that most fascinating of all nicknames
which, even years later when I heard it
applied to New York, still retained
that boyhood association with you.

Friday nights, huddled under blankets
in rickety wooden bleachers on the home side
of the field, we waited, adoring, faithful devotees,
for that supreme moment when you would take
the handoff, almost disappear in a crowd of linemen,
then, springing free of their clutches, miraculously
and joyfully explode into the secondary, racing
past linebackers and defensive backs, coasting
on the fanatical wave of our shouting
the last few strides into the end zone.

But then your life stopped short, like a blocked punt,
as frame-frozen as those grainy films coaches
endlessly review to try to figure out why
the game plan broke down. You didn't marry the girl,
you didn't get the college scholarship, you didn't,
so far as we knew, even find a regular job.
By the time I became a senior, and number two
center, you were just another washed-up jock,
as forgotten as last year's headline.
Sometimes we'd see you in the crowd,
never cheering, just watching, brooding,
more often than not disapprovingly,
even contemptuously, as the underclassmen,
one of them wearing your old number,
now claimed the field, the fans, the game.

I never knew about the drinking
until I read of your death in the paper:
an event even stranger, more mysterious,
than your nickname or those Friday night moves.
Nobody learned what started the fire,
or where the night watchman had been,
only that you, drunk again, had been arrested
and thrown into the town jail, its only prisoner
that fateful night, and that you died of suffocation
before the firemen could extinguish the blaze.
When they found your body it was still
lying on the cot, limp as a dressing room in defeat,
emptied of all that former speed and energy
and grace, and locked in a grasp heavier,
and more certain, than any linebacker's or safety's,
Life and Death being the only opponents
you couldn't duck, stiff-arm, or juke.

Letter from an Old Teammate

Best friends, for two years
we were starters, I at quarterback,
you the center.

We never were champions,
but in that macho, never-say-die
world of festering manhood,
for even the smallest cheer or hug,
we endured suffocating two-a-days
in an airless Mississippi August
that sucked the best juices
from our tender souls;
season-long aches and bruises
inflicted by the fierce, unforgiving
blocks and tackles of linebackers;
the threat of lifetime injury
from the vulgar, screaming commands
of insane coaches who thought
of fumbles as the worst kind
of indecent exposure.

And, yes, the crude, endless jokes
about assuming the doggie position,
playing with each other's genitals,
the "hump-hump" of signal calling,
and our being married.

We were, I guess,
lovers of sorts — had to be,
to make it through those grueling practices
and those frigid Friday nights
with near-empty stands.
Were we just lucky?
Or was it all that time we spent
on the sidelines perfecting our snap
while the other players
were just screwing around
or ogling the cheerleaders?
Whatever the case,
we played twenty games together
and never once mishandled an exchange.

Yesterday my wife filed for divorce.
For ten years we tried to get
our signals right and, Lord knows,
it wasn't from want of practice.
But we just never could
adapt to each other's moves.
And even the best of dreams —
the fly pattern for the end zone,
the sideline out, the fullback draw
on third and long, the pitchout
around end — is doomed to fail
if the exchange is lost.

The exchange is everything.
But love is a different kind
of exchange, and marriage another
kind of game, one I now know
that football, except for the bruises,
failed to prepare me for.

So tonight, old buddy, I sit
in a lonely, empty dressing room,
where there are no cheers, no victory,
no parade. Just an an old, tired,
beatup quarterback, wondering who or what
to blame for the busted play.

Big Alex

For Alex Clinton

Last Saturday,
from high in Houck Stadium,
I watched you, number 98,
lift and fling opposing linemen
like confetti, chase and crush
the quarterback to the ground,
raise your arms in triumph
toward the sky.

Today, staring at the floor,
nervously folding and unfolding
your hands, you recount,
in pained, hushed tone,
an incident from your past:
"Get down on your knees, nigger boy.
I'd just as soon shoot you
as have you lick these dirty boots."
I feel the cold barrel
against your flesh. I know,
with you, the certainty of death.
I marvel that your gentleness,
gentle giant, could survive
such spearing.

Next Saturday I'll comprehend
your quickened fury,
your tireless drive, your greatness,
and I'll cheer more and more loudly,
loudest of all.

Willie Taylor, Noseguard

When I hear silly talk
of killer instinct
and the necessity
of hating your opponent,

I recall Willie Taylor,
all-conference noseguard,
and remember how,
Saturday after Saturday,
he would start every game
by sticking his hand
across the line of scrimmage
and shaking hands
with the center
he was supposed to hate
that day.

It always struck me
as a way of saying,
I'm good, you're good,
and about three hours from now
we'll know who's best.

Then, for the rest of the game
the two of them would engage
in hand-to-hand, no-holds-barred,
gouge-as-gouge-can
trench warfare.

Afterward the two
exhausted battlers
would shake hands again,
sometimes even hug — acknowledgment
that with weaker opponents
they'd both be just average jocks,
riding the end of the bench
and wondering why they weren't
getting more playing time.

The Way to Watch a Football Game

Not from a reserved seat
in the brightly lit stadium,
wrapped in the blanket
of the anonymous crowd,
with the players
lined and numbered in place
like pieces on a chess board
or monotonous, repetitive figures
in a video game.

But, say, from the alley
that runs behind the stadium,
standing in the dark,
peering through the fence
and thickly planted trees
intended to obscure the view
of those who refuse to pay
the price of conformity.

Watch the quarterback
lodge the ball in the branches
of a maple tree.
Watch the runner turn end
to disappear in a rush
of moving leaves.
Look for him to reappear
beyond the next tree.
He may or may not.
Watch the defenders
play hide-and-seek
among the high hedges.
Read the tackle from the roar
of the largely invisible crowd.
Watch the receiver
leaping for the rising moon.

You won't need
to see the scoreboard.
You already know
who's won.

Lone Kicker

His season is over,
third losing one in a row,
but on this cold December day,
his sole companion
a mechanical holder,
the only sound the heavy thud
of foot against ball,
he sends kick after kick,
20, 30, 40 yards,
high and true
toward the goal posts.

Next year
will be different.
These empty stands
will be filled
with cheering fans,
on their feet,
leaning into the final seconds
of the crucial game,
as he puts his foot
to the game-winning,
conference-clinching,
bowl-securing
field goal.

Even in the bitter cold
of this winter day
he can already feel
the warm, welcome press
of his teammates
racing onto the field,
pummeling him to the ground.

THE POLE VAULTER
AND OTHER HEROES

Saturday Night Wrestling

Almost every Saturday night, after supper,
we would gather, six or eight of us,
boys and men, on the front porch
of the Crossroads general store
and walk to Miss Nan Scott's house,
welcomed there to watch
the first television set in the community.
Usually we stuck to the gravel road,
talking and laughing as we walked,
waving at the passing cars headed
for a Saturday night in town,
but when there was a full moon to light
our way, we could take the shortcut
through Barmore Agnew's pasture
in order to arrive early enough
to watch an episode of *Dragnet*.

But we had come for wrestling,
and our long hike was well rewarded
when Vern Gagne took on Dick the Bruiser
or, better, if we chanced to pick a night
when Lou Thesz, the handsome,
clean-cut, all-American favorite,
triumphed over Gorgeous George,
whose marceled blond hair, sequined orchid robes,
and perfumed, officious style,
even diminished in black and white,
offended not just Southern boys but a whole nation.
We huddled around the small screen,
Miss Scott joining the rest of us in cheering
the muscular, masculine Thesz
and booing his dandy, effeminate opponent.
And such was our hysteria and hate,
poor, innocent underdogs though we were,
that it would not have altered our rabid
sympathies one bit could we have known
that Thesz would live to be an old man,
filthy rich, skiing the slopes of St. Moritz
and watching sailboats from his bay-front
*

condominium on Chesapeake Bay,
while George, money gone, marriages failed,
liver and kidneys shot from drinking,
a cough constant and uncontrolled,
would be dead of a heart attack at 48.

Requital

Old man.
I watch you straddle
the barbed fence,
ache yourself over,
limp through bitterweeds
and piles of manure
to the pond below.

I follow,
wrestling with fishing rods
and tackle box,
dutiful son
if no longer a child,
fitting my path once more
to the diminishing measure
of your step.

We are different now,
you see that as well as I.
Still, each year we return
to this place to enact
the ancient ritual.

Today, though,
I leave the fishing to you:
I have other game to catch.
Careless of the lure
bouncing quietly on the water,
I watch you across the narrow lake
and recall how once there was
between us more than water,
a gulf too wide for casting.

But that was long ago:
today I sit idly
and trace my sinking youth
in the wrinkled absolution
of your face, grateful
for the armistice of age,
the peace that somehow survives
the rage of passion and regret.

Like that bass there,
which you now lead thrashing
across the violent wave
and lift, with still strong
and steady hands, into
the splendid, sun-splashed air.

.

Tenure Track

Any day, around 4 or 4:30,
you can find us here,
exiting our parked cars
and climbing the hill
to the university track,
where, singly or in pairs or threesomes,
wearing loose-fitting sweats
to hide our weight and wrinkles,
we circle the outside lanes
in a leisurely walk or a limping jog,
talking as we go:
about the new admissions policy,
the new provost, the new fieldhouse,
how the campus situation
was much better years ago.

I'm Wilson, from History.
Some days I jog alone,
but more often with Hutchinson,
from English, and McGregor, from Art.
We leave the inside lanes open
for the faster runners —
members of the track teams,
men's and women's,
and a few younger professors,
unfriendly and untenured,
who continually check their watches,
then sprint as if in pursuit
of a future that has no patience
with patience.

Once or twice a week
these runners are joined by Lawson,
my first-year colleague in History,
a detestable and obsessive new historicist
who reads race, class, or gender
into every event and text,
as he punctuates his ten-mile road run
with a few laps around the track.
*

Such hubris! Sweeping into and out
of the stadium in long, smooth strides,
breathing easily, scarcely
even breaking a sweat,
unspeaking as he laps us older profs.

Today the mischief and resentment
in me will not be repressed.
Precisely timing my final lap
just as Lawson moves up to pass me
once again, I break into a full sprint,
feel young again as I widen the distance
between us. When I cross the finish line,
he is a good fifty yards behind,
not even knowing he has lost a race.
By the time he catches up
I'll already be casually toweling off
and heading for my car. This time
I might even condescend to speak.

Autumn at Woodland Hills Country Club

Putts hang on doubting faces,
and wayward drives bogey the heart
beside spreading hazards of sand and rough.

Shouting summer dreams
lie strangely mocked beneath
the protracted whine of electric carts.

This is the season of anxious men,
nervously flitting from green
to green, in furious pursuit
of ancient springtime's eagled promise.

This is the season of desperate men,
clubhouse bravado and patio laughter
now chilled by stripped skeletons
rising like specters above fading fairways.

This is the season of angry men.
Only the leaves are patient,
orange and red and yellow,
burrowing quietly in ditch and hedge
to await a sure rejuvenation.

But the players,
fat, and breathless,
and older than they know,
one by one,
flail and flail their mute protest
against the immovable earth,
the snowy onslaught of winter.

Secretariat

Big Red.

A non-athlete, some say,
because he was not human.

A bolt of lightning
splitting the air.

A roaring tornado
devouring earth.

A swooping hawk
scattering smaller birds.

A moving mountain
dwarfing fading hills.

But no super athlete
is human.

And where were you
when the fiery god came down
to do his triple dance
before the startled gaze
of mortal men?

The Pole Vaulter

For L. D. Brodsky

The pole vaulter, like the poet,
depends on concentration, skill, vision.

See him there, at the end of the runway,
in those last compacted moments
before the approach,
strategically gauging the wind,
the distance, the speed of the track,
isolating himself from the pop
of the starter's gun, the blur
of sprinters racing past, the roar
of the crowd, burrowing within himself
for the strength and inspiration and will
required for the challenge.

Now centered, poised for takeoff,
and rocking, almost imperceptibly,
heel to toe, heel to toe,
he lifts the pole and moves
forward, gaining speed, fixing his gaze
on that single point of time and space
at the end of the runway, where,
grounded in the earth
to which he must return,
he will lift off and rise, rise,
rise, feet first, pulling legs,
heart, head, arms, eyes after.
Clearing the bar, breathless,
momentarily balanced between heaven
and earth, and just before the free fall
of gravity overtakes and pulls him back,
he catches the briefest glimpse
of pure blue sky, emptied of any trace
of cloud or shadow.

Thus poets long, time and time again,
for that moment when they plant their pen
to page and eagerly wait
for the buoyancy of their imagination
and the sweat of their labor
to vault them, on soaring words,
into a sky-blue heaven
of their own making, floating free.

Just now — don't miss it —
take your mind off the shot-putter
and the jumper and the miler
and watch him there again,
readying for his next attempt,
nervously walking about,
staring down the narrow runway,
straining to see, in his mind's eye,
the deed already done.

Martina: Last Wimbledon

For Laurie

A whole generation
followed you, proud and defiant,
out of the closet
to this hallowed center court.

Woman, lover, champion,
you taught us all, gay or straight,
another measure of grace
and beauty and courage.

Once, feeling rage
and rejection, you thought
the fans loved Chrissy more.
And so they did.

But that was then, her moment.
This is now, yours:
a different colored wallpaper
pasted on the walls of tradition.

This day belongs to history,
not tennis, and watching,
we feel the earth shift, balance,
as subtext now becomes text.

The crowd cheers your greatness.
Royalty bends its knee.
You mark the moment with a blade of grass,
knowing your time, and ours, has come.

Robert Frost, Runner

I

Shovel beneath the shock of white hair,
cold and pure as the snow that masks
the rocky New England soil.

Scan the lines and slope of the craggy face,
grief-tough and solid as birches
thronging a hillside in New Hampshire or Vermont.

Stare into the fierce, savage eyes
that flame, in anger or hurt,
like rebellious stars in the blackest night.

And know then the tenacious heart
that dared embrace the bleakest winter truth
and still find cause for joy, beauty, love,
forgiveness of man and God.

Whence came such paradox of delight
and wisdom, such strength of will,
that toughness of the skeptic's mind
and passion of the lover's heart
that enabled you to outlast
the long years of neglect
and the bitter jealousy of lesser poets?
For that, we must spade deeper
than a Derry pasture or apple orchard,
across a continent, in fact,
and a lifetime.

II

San Francisco, 1884.
Daily, through the cobbled streets,
a young boy runs with his father,
whose body is drained and wasting away
with consumption.

Day after day, up and down hills,
feet pounding the pavement, lungs gasping air,
heart straining for strength,
they run. The boy knows, with the father,
it is a race they cannot win.
Yet still they run.

The boy stretches his stride,
struggles to keep pace,
willing his own strength and breath
into the declining body of the man.

Some days they run to the beach,
where the boy sits on the shore,
his father's clothes lying beside him,
and watches the father swim away from him,
farther and farther out,
sees him disappear beyond the breakers,
fearing, knowing, that one day
he will fall over the edge of the earth,
never to return.

Neither, of course, does the boy.
In his place stands the future poet,
alien and alone on the cold Pacific sand,
feeling vast love and pity
for all fathers, all sons,
runners all.

Running: Cape Girardeau, November 1993

Running is good in any season,
but best in that wafer-thin
slice of time when autumn, peaking,
tops a hill and catches its breath
in a cornucopia of color before coasting
downhill to winter.

The time of day images the season.
The sun waits just above the treetops
to receive the baton from a sky of blue
before beginning the final leg of descent.
Light, gold-tinted by the lingering leaves,
slants across the still-green grass,
blinding the eye on its way to dark.

I take my dog Nellie,
a domesticated beagle delirious
from cabin fever. Innocent of time,
she leaps at the door as I put on
sweats and shoes, barks with glee
as we leave the house, races on ahead
as we cut through a neighbor's yard
to reach the cross country trail
winding through the woods.

On the track I settle into a steady jog,
balancing Nellie's youthful spasms of desire
with the slowing rhythm of middle age.
Nose to the ground, scent sharpened
by the cold, she passionately explores
pasture, culvert, creek, woods, heedless
of my call to stay. Doubling back, fetching
me from a distance, she is puzzled
by my reluctance to hurry, bids me sprint,
engorge with her the whole of nature
in one ravenous bite.

But knowing now the patience of days
and seasons, contented with them,
I hold my slow and easy pace,
savoring every morsel of delight:
layered leaves that color and perfume
the ground, lattices of light and shadow
that clock my steps, blue sky
disappearing in gray,
my breath, soul, painting the air
with traces of silver smoke.

By now Nellie is nowhere to be seen,
but the second time around the track,
darkness overtaking us,
she'll be running at my heels,
willingly matching her pace to mine.

HALF-COURT ADVANTAGE

Basketball Suite

I: Point Guard

It all begins with me.
I call the plays,
dribble and dish,
a conductor
wielding the baton,
a little socialist
spreading the wealth.
You have a hot hand,
I'll get you the rock.
You left your game at home
with your sweetie,
you won't touch leather tonight.
Peel off the pick,
the ball will already be there
for you, waiting
to be plucked,
huge and sweetest of fruits,
off the screener's shoulder.
Post up inside,
the bounce pass
will find your hands
like a lost puppy.
Put the defender on your hip,
look for manna
falling from heaven.
I live to drive the lane,
scoop it between bodies
or hang the moon
for a slam dunk.
And if you're going to guard me
you'd better know this,
don't ever try to run with me
in the open court.
When I'm loose and grooving
it's now you see it, now you don't,
change hands, behind the back,
between the legs,
*

look right and throw left,
the crowd will tell you
where I've gone.

II: Center

They call me the Enforcer.
I never smile.
I live in the paint,
which I own
like my girlfriend's pussy.

The game is decided
at my table,
winner take all.

I can score,
turnaround jumpers,
baby hooks, tip-ins,
an occasional slam,
but boarding is my game.
When the shot goes up,
get ready to rumble.
I'll block out, hold,
gouge, throw an elbow,
whatever it takes.

On defense
my job is to create chaos
out of order.
A mad dog
defending my turf.
Bring your shit into my house,
I'll plant it three rows deep
in the stands.
And put your ass
on the floor
so you won't forget.

If you want flash and show,
look to the pretty boys
out front.
If you want results
on the scoreboard,
bring it underneath
where the men get
down and dirty.

III: Quick Forward

I'm at home anywhere,
outside or inside,
can do it all,
work over the top
or take it down
among the trees,
pass, shoot,
or put it on the floor.
A long, lean, in-your-face
flying machine.

Crowd me too much,
I'll blow past you
for a power dunk,
back off,
I'll burn you
with a jumper.

Match my quickness,
I'll post you down low,
match my size,
you'll spend the night
reading my name
on the back of my jersey.

Talk all the trash
you want.
I'll answer with my moves.

IV: Power Forward

Sometimes I'm invisible
during the game,
but you'll always find
my numbers in the box score.
I come to play.

I'm the in-betweener.
Not huge and dominant enough
to be an intimidator
or small and quick enough
to make the highlight films,
I know my role,
play within myself,
block out, help out on defense,
pick up the garbage
around the basket.

Coaches love me.
I work hard, give my all,
never quit,
my glory is the team.
Fans may not know my name,
but they can read it
on the trophy.

V: Shooting Guard

My job is to score.
I make nets dance
like cheerleaders' skirts.

When I'm in the zone
you can take it to the bank.

A loner and drifter,
I hate crowds,
hang out in the open spaces
*

on the wing
or in the deep corner,
a frontier sharpshooter
who can gun down
an opponent's rally,
ambush its heart,
with another long-range bullet.
I have no fear,
no conscience.
Opponents hate me,
teammates envy
my smooth, fluid stroke.
My coach loves me
and hates me.

But I'm the darling
of the fans.
Look for my autograph
in the referee's uplifted arms
and the row of treys
taped to the arena wall.

Get me the ball
and clear out.
You can ride this train
to the Promised Land.

Girls' Basketball, 1950s Style

Girls' basketball.
Not *women's*. Not in the 1950s.
That would come later,
and later still in Baldwyn, Mississippi.

Half-court play only,
forwards on this end, guards on that.
Everyone a specialist, virginal.
Unlike boys, who can do it all.

Win or lose,
you must never, never,
cross the dividing line.
Know your place.

Two dribbles only.
Don't sweat.
Sit out the menstrual cycle.
Save your cherry for your husband.

Cradle the ball in your arms
like a baby.
Swish two-handed set shots.
But never dream of dunking.

Babe McCarthy

You gotta come out at 'em
like a bitin' sow, he said.
Let's cloud up
and rain all over 'em, he said.
The sun don't shine
on the same dog's butt ever' day, he said.
But long before he became
the legendary ABA coach
known as "Magnolia Mouth"
for his honeyed Southern drawl
and down-home sayings,
he had coached at Mississippi State,
snatched four SEC championships
from Adolph Rupp's greedy grasp,
incurred the anger and threats
of Governor Ross Barnett
and the White Citizens' Council
by slipping his white boys
out of the state to play
for the first time against blacks.

And before that he coached
the Baldwyn High School Bearcats
to the 1948 Mississippi state championship.
I was a fifth grader that year,
watching from the stands
as players I knew
and passed on the school yard every day
blossomed suddenly into heroes.
My family listened excitedly
to the broadcast of the final game
on the Philco radio that usually sat
on top of the refrigerator
so Mama could hear *Stella Dallas*
and her other soap operas
while she worked in the kitchen,
confiscated this day and moved
to the living room so the whole family
could follow the game.
*

One of the Bearcats, Thomas Morris,
nicknamed "Bucket,"
was almost family, his brother
being married to my oldest sister;
and another, Herman Suratt,
had dated my other sister for a time.
The championship was all the sweeter
because we beat our archrival, Booneville,
in the tournament finals.

Babe died in 1975 of colon cancer,
not long after he was selected,
for the second time,
as the ABA Coach of the Year.
He was only 51 years old,
but I feel sure he faced death
as confidently and fearlessly
as he did opposing teams and politicians.
Why panic at five in the mornin'
because it's still dark out? he said.

In Memoriam: For Gerald Caveness

Coaching is a young man's profession.
All coaches know that,
so most of them early on
go into insurance, become principals,
open sporting goods stores.
But not you.
Even after the first heart attack
sent you into sudden death,
you continued to coach.
I still see you at the edge of the court,
anxiously seated on a folding chair,
leaning into the action,
towel dangling in your hand,
your piercing eagle eyes searching for . . . what?
What was it in the game, beyond the game,
that so engrossed that rapt attention?
That would not let you
heed the advice of wife, doctors, friends,
and retire from the sport?

It wasn't the winning, as many believed.
You had enough victories for two lifetimes:
six state championships,
Coach of the Year honors,
election to state and regional halls of fame,
more trophies and plaques
than you could even recall.
Your teams are still the stuff of legend
in those tiny communities
scattered across northeast Mississippi,
even in Jackson, the state capital,
where year after year in the huge Coliseum
your anonymous farm- and small-town boys
defeated and frequently embarrassed
the big-school favorites
loaded with superstars on their way
to Ole Miss, Mississippi State, or Memphis State.

What then, if not the success,
the recognition, the fame,
brought you back to those bandbox gyms,
those smelly, cramped dressing rooms,
those endless, late-night bus rides,
again and again and again?

Once I thought I had a clue. It was 1964;
your New Site Royals had just lost in the finals
of the Baldwyn Christmas Tournament.
They had played four nights in a row,
the championship game lasting three overtimes.
That same night, after the postgame talk
and the long bus ride home,
you locked the doors of the gym
and kept parents and girlfriends waiting until 12:30 a.m.
while you drilled the team on its motion offense.

You were an artist, and your team's play
carried your signature as visibly
as a painter's name in the corner of the canvas.
Your tools were discipline, effort, teamwork —
and an unbending conviction
that the notion of mankind's imperfectability
did not apply within the boundaries
of your domain.
You believed that any team of five individuals,
whatever the degree of talent,
could still, through sheer exercise
of grit and grind and savvy,
sustain perfection for at least four quarters
of eight minutes each.
And not only could but by God would
if they ever hoped to play for Gerald Caveness.
And that's what you demanded
at the end of that eagle gaze:
players setting the hard pick,
blocking the jumper off the boards,
taking only the good shot,
*

hitting the open man,
helping out on defense.
You practiced so long the players
heard your voice in their sleep:
"Play smart! Play tough! Above all, be patient!
Use each possession not only to score
but to wear down the opposition.
Make them think that when they miss a shot,
they'll never get the ball back.
Pass and cut, pass and cut,
keep moving without the ball.
Watch for the frustration, the quit,
in their eyes."
And while they slept, you stayed awake,
watching game films, studying opponents,
diagramming x's and o's,
never doubting that a game plan
could be choreographed and executed as precisely
as a cheerleader's sideline routine.

But life cannot be choreographed
like game strategy.
When the second heart attack came,
even you, master of the delay game,
who always taught that time was an ally,
were forced to concede that the game clock
had finally, cruelly, expired.
And this time there would be no overtime.
So you fished, and watched games on TV
and prepared the last x's and o's for your family,
and waited for the Referee's final whistle.

The doctors reported
you were born with a bad heart.
Not so: rather, you had given so much
of your heart to others,
and to the game you loved,
that there was so little left over for yourself.
On the day of your funeral
*

we all gathered to pay homage:
family, former players, fellow coaches,
sportswriters, admiring fans.
As we listened to eulogies and praises,
many nodded in agreement or softly whispered amens;
but mostly we just huddled quietly
and remembered — the teams, the players,
the big games, the big plays.
Someone recalled the pronouncement
a few years earlier by a hill farmer,
leaving a movie theater in Tupelo
after viewing *Hoosiers*:
"Hell," he said to no one in particular,
"they made the movie about the wrong man.
Gerald Caveness at New Site did that,
not once, but five years in a row!"
All the way to the cemetery and back
we gave thanks for you, Coach Caveness,
secular priest of the hardwood,
who showed us all that basketball,
rightly played,
is just another way of imaging the world
as God himself intended it to work
on the day He fashioned the globe
into the first roundball
and tossed it into the heavens
toward a distant goal.

On the Death of the Evansville University Basketball Team in a Plane Crash, December 13, 1977

And now we know
why coaches rage,
kick benches,
curse rivals and referees.

Here, on this corpse-strewn hill
where grief smothers hope
with an obscene fog,
finality the only prize,
the orphaned heart knows
that every contest is do or die,
that all opponents are Death
masquerading in school colors,
that each previous season is
mere preliminary for encounter
with this last, bitter cup.

Yet we would not have it so,
it must not be so:
man is not made for death.
Cry foul. Shriek protest.
Claim a violation.
Even in losing, dying,
herald the perfect play.

So scream, all-knowing coaches,
admonishing priests, scream.
Swear, chew asses, make us work.
Never quit.
What else sustains
in nights when dreams
plummet downward in darkness
to question the betraying earth?

Oldtimer

Leaving the campus,
heading north on Henderson,
I brake to allow
an elderly man
to cross the street.

He cautiously steps
off the curb, walks
slowly but steadily,
confidently
claiming the right of way
even here
in the middle of the block.

Glancing back
as I drive on,
I recognize him
as Jack Behrens,
a retired colleague,
remembered by most
as a dedicated and successful
educator and administrator,
but by some
as the player who scored
the winning basket
in SEMO's only
national championship
victory.

Memories more numerous
than the cars
on this busy street
come streaming toward me.
Of the colleague
I worked with
for twenty years.
Of the countless conferences
and board meetings
and committee sessions
*

we attended.
Of the trip we once made
to Memphis
on university business.
Of our many conversations
about school, politics, sports,
family.

But mostly
his joyous recollection
of that final shot
that decided
a basketball game
in 1943:
Kansas City,
Municipal Auditorium,
thirty-two teams,
now reduced to two.
Game tied 32-32,
Maryville in possession
with fifteen seconds left.
"I had been moved to forward
because Pug Russell was hurt,
so when they shot and missed
I cut out for the basket.
Bidewell got the rebound,
threw it to Anderson on the wing,
who made a long pass
downcourt to me.
I took a couple of dribbles
toward the goal
but when I glanced at the clock
I saw there were only
a couple of seconds left.
So I stopped at the top
of the free throw circle
and took a two-handed set shot.
I knew immediately
it was going in.
*

I can still feel how perfect it felt
leaving my hands
and still see the ball swishing the net.
I grabbed the ball
and kept it for forty years."

I was a four-year-old child
in Mississippi
when that shot went in,
and I never played
in any college game,
much less one
for a national championship.
But I've admired that ball
nestling quietly
in a trophy case,
and I can see it swishing the net,
even now, just as though
I had been there,
one of that cheering crowd.

Comeback

Yesterday
your best friend called
from St. Louis, reporting
that he was checking into the hospital
for his second angioplasty.
He had already concluded that this one
wouldn't work either, that eventually
he would need the bypass.
He was remarkably accepting,
even calm and stoical, about the situation.
"It comes to all of us," he said.
"Now it's my turn."

Last night
you dreamed of your father:
it was a memory of childhood,
except that your father was the cancer-ravaged
ghost you remembered at the end.

Today you played
your weekly pickup game
with your buddies, who remarked
that your play was extraordinarily fierce
and competitive for a friendly game.
They never saw the skeleton
clinging to your back, its arms
wrapped in a strangle hold about your neck,
its gaping mouth pressed to your ear,
whispering in a ghastly and taunting voice,
"Drive! Drive! Drive!"

Pick and Roll

For Mark Haertling

Twenty years ago, a mere teenager,
you hit a buzzer-beater from the top
of the key to deprive my AAU team
of a city championship.
"Mr. Clutch," the next day's headline
proclaimed you, and you've never
let me forget it, especially each
Christmas vacation, when many
of my former players and your teammates
return home and join us at the Rec Center
for a friendly game of remembering.
"Hey, Coach, watch this," you call,
and I see you again at the top of the key,
older now, fatter, and grinning this time
as the ball once more swishes the net.
"Mr. Clutch," you remind me, twisting
the knife of defeat yet again
in my aching, regretful heart.

But today, Mark, all is forgiven.
On this day, in a pickup game, at age 52,
it was I who had the hot hand,
and you fed me and fed me:
for the corner jumper, the swinging hook
across the lane, the left-handed reverse
layup, the high lob on the back door cut.
And best of all that pick and roll,
the ball floating unexpectedly into my vision
and hanging there just above my head
like a large, tamed bird which I
enfolded in grateful hands and gently, deftly,
guided home to roost.

To an Athlete Dying Old

Suited,
briefcase in hand,
he stops, as always,
beside playground voices
going three on three.

Far beyond
his flabby muscles
and spreading paunch
a basketball springs alive once more,
bouncing, bouncing, bouncing,
to images of ideal forms:

Between the legs,
behind the back,
body spinning, driving,
leaping, hanging in air,
the ball banking off the board
and swishing the net
in perfect fulfillment.

Walking on,
he is keenly aware
he has not smelled
his own body-sweat in weeks.

Scoring

Time after time
my youthful opponent slides outside,
takes a pass at the top of the key,
and buries an 18-foot jumper.

I crowd him with as much hustle
as my middle-aged body can command,
but he's too lean and quick.
Even were I not so old and slow,
there'd be no stopping him.
He's in the zone.

Crowding him more, I feel
my outstretched hand graze
against his silken crotch
as he hits the floor
after releasing another swisher.

Damn! He has a hard-on!
No wonder I can't guard the bastard!

That was the exact moment
when I realized why I had never been,
never would be, a jock.

Watching the Christmas Tournament with an Old Friend

For Bob Talley

Clearly
we've both accepted
the fact
that we're going to see
each other
just once a year,
at this annual high school
Christmas tournament.

And if we ever decide
not to attend these games,
I guess we won't see
each other at all.

From our midcourt seats
we watch the marathon
of games flow
up and down the court,
the same teams
we've watched for years,
the same school colors,
the same cheerleaders' yells,
the same crowd response
to buzzer beaters
and turnovers,
the same screaming
at officials' calls
by irate coaches,
the same ecstasy and heartbreak
over victory and defeat.

Even some
of the players' names
are the same:
three rows below us
a grandfather
*

whose retired jersey
now hangs on the wall
of this arena
watches his grandson
hit a clutch pull-up jumper
and retreat down the court,
pumping his fist
into the air.

We follow the games,
admire the players' moves,
watch the scoreboard —
but mostly talk:
about our wives
and children and grandchildren
(you have a new one this year),
about players and teams
we remember
from previous tournaments,
about kids we used to coach
in church league and AAU,
about retirement
and your golf game
and my writing.

Each year
the coaches are younger,
some just kids,
the players more athletic
and talented,
the uniform pants
much longer,
but the game itself
still clocks down
to essences,
outlasting changing patterns
and the passing
of the years.

Like a long friendship,
ever enduring, still cherished,
and perpetually renewed.

Basketball at 65

"Are you still
playing basketball?"
my sister asked,
during a recent visit.

"Yes," I told her,
"when my knees will allow."

"You don't play full court, do you?"

"No. Just half-court."

Then, on second thought:

"Actually we don't play
half-court either;
we usually just stand
in one place
and hope the ball
will come to us."

Last Sneaks

For years now I've thought
every pair of sneakers
I buy is bound to be
the last.

But here I am again,
outfitting myself
with another new pair
for the biweekly pickup game
I play with the old farts.

My favorites are still
the Converse canvas hightops
that I used into my thirties,
grudgingly giving them up
only when my buddies told me,
"If you don't buy yourself
some different shoes,
we're going to quit
playing with you.
We're ashamed to be seen
on the same court with you."

Funny, at the time
we were all still wearing
the tight short shorts
that bespoke the fifties
even before we put up
the first one-handed set shot.

Still, I heeded the warning
and for the past thirty years,
I've worn Wilsons, Adidas,
Reeboks, New Balances,
and a dozen other brands,
even Nikes before Michael Jordan
outsourced his conscience to Asia.

But this pair, I think,
will indeed be my last.
Two back surgeries
and a bum knee
scream at me louder
than any old coach,
telling me it's time to retire.
So maybe I will.

Then again,
maybe I won't.

Half-Court Advantage

For teammates Terry Begley,
Frank Chong, and Jim Hillin

Not every diminishment, thankfully,
is final. The body moves slower now,
in comic mimicry of its early grace;
aches more, takes longer and longer
to recover. Still, once, twice,
three times a week, we come
to this place to match our skill,
four on four, against younger opponents.

After twenty years of playground challenges,
only our lovers read our moves as well.
We each know our role, our limits:
Jim arches long jumpers
from the top of the key;
Frank threads needle passes
and scoop shots past flailing
arms and legs; Terry cans sweeping
hooks moving right and left;
I'm the board and garbage man,
working the low post.

Often now we're overmatched,
but we've learned the half-court game
negates speed and lightness,
rewards craftiness and desire:
the backdoor move, blocking out,
the pick and roll, an intentional foul.
Occasionally we win, making them take it,
though, this late in the season,
we understand that's unimportant.

What matters in this remaining space,
where all contests are played close
to the ground, is the sound and rhythm
of ball on pavement, the flow
of the moment, press of flesh on flesh,
high-five satisfaction of sweat and fatigue
*

and togetherness. Here we find our best,
learn again the strategy of survival,
practice the art of staying alive.

Later, bruised and exhausted,
wrapped around the water fountain,
we hear someone call, "One more game?"
None of us says no.

BIOGRAPHICAL NOTE

Robert Hamblin is Professor of English and Director of the Center for Faulkner Studies at Southeast Missouri State University. A native of Mississippi, he holds degrees from Northeast Mississippi Community College, Delta State University, and the University of Mississippi. A former athlete and coach, he regularly teaches a course in sport literature and served for two decades as the poetry editor for *Aethlon: The Journal of Sport Literature*.

OTHER POETRY AND SHORT FICTIONS AVAILABLE FROM TIME BEING BOOKS

866-840-4334
HTTP://WWW.TIMEBEING.COM

Harry James Cargas (editor)
Telling the Tale: A Tribute to Elie Wiesel on the Occasion of His 65th Birthday — Essays, Reflections, and Poems

Judith Chalmer
Out of History's Junk Jar: Poems of a Mixed Inheritance

Gerald Early
How the War in the Streets Is Won: Poems on the Quest of Love and Faith

Gary Fincke
Blood Ties: Working-Class Poems

Charles Adés Fishman
Chopin's Piano

CB Follett
Hold and Release

Albert Goldbarth
A Lineage of Ragpickers, Songpluckers, Elegiasts & Jewelers: Selected Poems of Jewish Family Life, 1973–1995

Robert Hamblin
From the Ground Up: Poems of One Southerner's Passage to Adulthood

William Heyen
Erika: Poems of the Holocaust
Falling from Heaven: Holocaust Poems of a Jew and a Gentile *(Brodsky and Heyen)*
The Host: Selected Poems, 1965–1990
Pterodactyl Rose: Poems of Ecology
Ribbons: The Gulf War — A Poem

Ted Hirschfield
German Requiem: Poems of the War and the Atonement of a Third Reich Child

866-840-4334
HTTP://WWW.TIMEBEING.COM

Virginia V. James Hlavsa
Waking October Leaves: Reanimations by a Small-Town Girl

Rodger Kamenetz
The Missing Jew: New and Selected Poems
Stuck: Poems Midlife

Norbert Krapf
Blue-Eyed Grass: Poems of Germany
Looking for God's Country
Somewhere in Southern Indiana: Poems of Midwestern Origins

Adrian C. Louis
Blood Thirsty Savages

Leo Luke Marcello
Nothing Grows in One Place Forever: Poems of a Sicilian American

Gardner McFall
The Pilot's Daughter

Joseph Meredith
Hunter's Moon: Poems from Boyhood to Manhood

Ben Milder
The Good Book Also Says . . . : Numerous Humorous Poems Inspired by
   the New Testament
The Good Book Says . . . : Light Verse to Illuminate the Old Testament
Love Is Funny, Love Is Sad
The Zoo You Never Gnu: A Mad Menagerie of Bizarre Beasts and Birds

Charles Muñoz
Fragments of a Myth: Modern Poems on Ancient Themes

Micheal O'Siadhail
The Gossamer Wall: Poems in Witness to the Holocaust

866-840-4334
HTTP://WWW.TIMEBEING.COM

Joseph Stanton
A Field Guide to the Wildlife of Suburban Oʻahu
Imaginary Museum: Poems on Art